Lympne Airport

IN OLD PHOTOGRAPHS

An aerial view of the airport at Lympne in the early 1930s, showing the three pairs of hangars and ancillary buildings, together with the concrete circle and the airport's identification marking. In the foreground are the 'fog condition signals' (white rectangles), the compass base (white circle) and HM Customs buildings to the left of the entrance road. (*Flight International*)

Lympne Airport

IN OLD PHOTOGRAPHS

Compiled by DAVID G. COLLYER

Alan Sutton Publishing Limited
Phoenix Mill · Far Thrupp
Stroud · Gloucestershire

First published 1992

**British Library Cataloguing
in Publication Data**

Collyer, David G.
  Lympne Airport in old photographs
  I. Title
  387-709422

ISBN 0-7509-0169-1

Typeset in 9/10 Sabon
Typesetting and origination by
Alan Sutton Publishing Limited.
Printed in Great Britain by
The Bath Press, Avon.

Half Title Page Photo
Refuelling an Armstrong–Whitworth Argosy of Imperial Airways in the 1930s required
some dexterity, as the petrol tanks were housed under the upper wing for safety. The
access to the open cockpit, which was separated from the passenger cabin, required the
use of long ladders by the mechanics as well as the crew, as seen in this photo of a routine
maintenance check being undertaken before the aircraft left Lympne for the Continent.

Contents

This DHC1 Chipmunk G-AOTM, a civilianized RAF trainer was photographed at Lympne Airport on 29 October 1956, with a French-built Jodel D149 F-BIZA and a visiting Douglas Dakota. This is a typical post-Second World War view of the activities at Lympne, with Skyways Dakotas G-AMSM and AMWW parked outside the hangar in the background together with a De Havilland Rapide. (R. Nicholls)

Introduction

The founding of and the continuing success of the airport at Lympne rested with its proximity to the Continent, as in March 1916 it was established as an Emergency Landing Ground for the Royal Flying Corps night fighters guarding the coast against the Zeppelin raiders. In January 1917 it was designated as No. 8 Aircraft Acceptance Park for the delivery of aircraft to, and reception from, France. Later aircraft were delivered in sections via its own railway line, to be modified, assembled and tested before being dispatched to the front line.

After 1918 Lympne was retained by the RAF as the point for the dispatch of service mail to the Continent, until August 1919. The airfield then became an HM Customs clearance point for air freight (1920), and embryo civil airliner services (1922) to the Continent were begun. A wireless station and an 'aerial lighthouse' were constructed. Thus it received many intersting British and foreign visiting aircraft, ranging from the minute 'Flying Flea' to the giant Handley Page HP42 airliners of Imperial Airways.

In 1923, 1924 and 1926 the series of Light Aviation Trials held at the airport was an attempt to encourage the establishment of flying clubs in the UK, and as part of the programme air racing was included. This became a tradition at the site until after the Second World War. Lympne was one of the control points for the King's Cup air races in 1929, and from 1922 a series of races were held, usually over the August Bank Holiday weekend, for a series of trophies, including the Folkestone Aero Trophy and the Wakefield Cup.

The location also encouraged long-distance flyers to use the airport as their departure or arrival point for their record attempts to Eastern Europe (1927), Australia (1931/4/6/7), South Africa (1927/31/2/6) and South America (1933/5), and pilots included both Amy Johnson and Jim Mollison, Kingsford Smith, C.W.A. Scott, Tommy Rose, Jean Batten, and a host of other well-known aviators.

In 1928 the inauguration of the East Kent Flying Club saw a start of the flying club operations at Lympne. This flying club was acquired by the world renowned Brooklands Group and renamed the Cinque Ports Flying Club in 1930. It became famous world-wide, as it trained large numbers of pilots from all parts of this country and abroad. The club also established its own engineering section where one club machine, the Currie Wot, was designed and built. Many foreign visitors attended the International Air Rallies until the outbreak of the Second World War.

The Royal Air Force returned in 1936, while the Empire Air Day of May 1937 recognized the importance of Lympne as the temporary home for two RAF squadrons (Nos. 21 and 34) after they had had to vacate their regular service aerodrome. Lympne was used by both the Royal Auxiliary Air Force and University Air Squadrons for training at their annual summer camps, and a flourishing Civil Air Guard was established in 1938 to train a reserve of RAF pilots for the forthcoming conflict.

In July 1939, Lympne became 'HMS Buzzard', a Royal Naval Air Station of the Fleet Air Arm, and September saw the evacuation of most of the flying club's machines. RAF Army Co-Operation squadrons from France returned there in May 1940, and Lympne temporarily hosted some of the French Air Force during the Dunkirk evacuation. After the reoccupation by the RAF, Lympne became a Biggin Hill Sector forward satellite fighter base of Fighter Command in daylight hours. During the summer of 1940, Lympne also succoured battle-damaged aircraft and wounded pilots, during the first weeks of the Battle of Britain.

Heavily bombed on numerous occasions during mid-August 1940, Lympne was temporarily closed and took no further part in the battle, but it soon reopened to host Spitfire, Typhoon and Hurricane squadrons operating over occupied Europe, for the Dieppe landings and during the build-up for D-Day. There were frequent arrivals of British and USAAF aircraft obliged to seek sanctuary when returning damaged, or short of fuel, from bomber raids over the Continent. Lympne also played its part during the V-1 attack of June–September 1944, both mounting strikes against the launching bases in the Pas de Calais, and countering the pilotless 'Doodle Bugs' themselves.

After the war, the Cinque Ports Flying Club was re-established in 1946, but soon folded, being followed by Kent Coast Flying Club which remained until 1953. Messrs Air Kruise's Trans-Channel Air Service, and Messrs Skyfotos aerial photography businesses were founded, the latter company gaining a worldwide reputation for their shipping photographs. As civil aviation struggled to achieve its pre-war status the activity at Lympne never quite reached its pre-war proportions, but air racing returned to Lympne for three brief years until 1948.

The commencement of the cross-Channel vehicle and passenger ferry service by Silver City Airways in 1948 saw flights with Bristol 170 Freighters to Le Touquet, and extended to Ostend before the move to their newly-built airport at Ferryfield, Lydd in 1954. Lympne was reopened in 1955, when commercial activity was continued by Messrs Skyways' coach-air service from London to Paris using Dakotas, and was later extended to Vichy, Lyon, Antwerp, and Brussels. After some financial difficulties, the company was re-formed in 1959, and in 1962 their new Avro 748 turboprop airliners were introduced on the Paris route, the Dakotas being converted for Skyways' air freight service.

The Cinque Ports Flying Club was re-established in 1964 and, together with Business Air Travel, encouraged light aviation. In 1967 the new all-weather concrete runway was used from Easter, with Skyways' airliner services being extended to Clement Ferrat, Montpelier, and Palma. In 1969 the new passenger terminal was opened, and some 300,000 passengers were using the airport each year.

However, another financial crisis saw Skyways taken over in a management buy-out in 1971, but their air freight service continued to flourish. Further financial problems led to a takeover by Dan Air, who operated from Lympne until they removed, with the flying club and other commercial operations, to Ferryfield in 1974. The name Lympne disappeared from the aviation scene in 1968 with the renaming of the location as Ashford Airport, in an attempt to enhance the status of the town; within six years, however, activity had been reduced to a parachute school and a joy-riding establishment. The site is now being developed as an industrial estate, although the occasional aircraft has still been known to land there – by mistake!

SECTION ONE

Royal Flying Corps
1916–1920

An aerial view of the grass airfield at Lympne so familiar to military pilots who arrived at this location while delivering their aircraft to France. By 1917 the permanent hangars had been erected in the south-western corner, to replace the temporary hangars and huts along the Lympne to Aldington road (B. Robertson)

Lympne originated as an Emergency Landing Ground for Home Defence night fighters operating against Zeppelins and Gothas heading for London. The airfield quickly acquired temporary hangars, technical buildings, and accommodation in the form of tents and wooden huts. In January 1917 the airfield became No. 8 Aircraft Acceptance Park for ferrying RFC aircraft to France; the construction of permanent hangars and buildings commenced and a railway spur was laid from Westenhanger Station.

The airfield was designated as a First Class Landing Ground in 1918 and was used by No. 53 Wing aircraft, including Sopwith Camels from No. 50 (H.D.) Squadron. In January 1918, No. 120 Bomber Squadron was formed there, together with The Day and Night Bombing and Observation School from May. The squadron flew their air mail service from Lympne to Cologne from July 1919 for a month, before returning to Hawkinge, which remained with the newly formed Royal Air Force, while Lympne reverted to civilian use, witnessing the start of commercial flying before the RAF relinquished its tenure at the end of 1920.

When Lympne became No. 8 Aircraft Acceptance Park in 1917 it hosted large numbers of RFC machines on delivery to France. After refuelling and mechanical checks, these would leave from the airfield for delivery to similar establishments on the Continent. As an aid to navigation, two large crosses were cut into the chalk on the cliffs at Folkestone and near Cap Gris Nez, to guide the ferry pilots in crossing the English Channel. (Capt. D.S. Glover, P.T.H. Green collection)

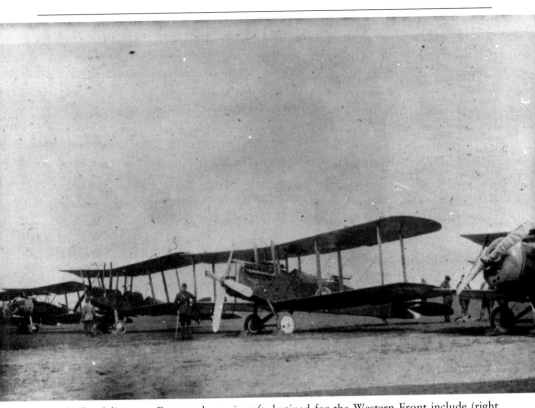

Ready for delivery to France, these aircraft destined for the Western Front include (right to left) a DH5 fighter-trainer, DH4 bomber, Royal Aircraft Factory-designed Be2E reconnaissance aircraft and a Sopwith 1½ Strutter light bomber. Before the erection of temporary hangars by October 1916, most of the routine maintenance work would have had to be undertaken by the mechanics in the open air. (Capt. D.S. Glover, P.T.H. Green collection)

The first of the three pairs of permanent hangars that were being erected at Lympne early in 1917, after the airfield had been designated as No. 8 Aircraft Acceptance Park. These 'General Service' sheds supplemented the eleven corrugated-iron sheds, workshops and offices which were situated on the south-west boundary. These nine hangars were eventually to be demolished after being severely damaged by fire as a result of enemy bombing on 15 August 1940, during the Battle of Britain. (B. Robertson)

Going Overseas. A Royal Aircraft Factory SE5A, the premier Royal Flying Corps fighter of 1917–18, heading towards France over one of the partially completed permanent hangars. The row of pine trees in the background is lining Otterpool Lane, across which was an extension of the airfield, while the airmen's camp was situated on allotments across the road to the south-west of the airfield. Lympne Castle served as the Officers Mess. (Capt. D.S. Glover, P.T.H. Green collection)

Ranged outside the newly completed hangars at Lympne *c.* 1917 are Bristol F2B two-seater Fighter (D7131) and two Royal Aircraft Factory designs, a Re8 reconnaissance aircraft and a Be12 fighter. The full range of storage available in the three pairs of hangars may be gauged from this view, used in post-war years by Imperial Airways airliners, visiting aircraft and those of the flying club. (Capt. D.S. Glover, P.T.H. Green collection)

This newly constructed Sopwith Dolphin fighter, seen here taking off for France, was among the wide range of aircraft which were delivered from Lympne to the four Aircraft Acceptance Parks near St Omer, by the RFC Ferry Flight. In the background can be seen some of the range of temporary canvas and timber Bessoneaux hangars, together with the workshops and other technical buildings that were erected along the Lympne–Aldington road. (Capt. D.S. Glover, P.T.H. Green collection)

This Italian-designed and built SIA 7B (5870) two-seater reconnaissance aircraft was the forerunner of many foreign aircraft to be seen at Lympne. It was photographed while *en route* from the Turin factory to Hounslow in 1917, piloted by Capt. Lauriati, who was accompanied by his mechanic and had landed at Lympne to refuel. It is not known, however, who the two civilians are. (Capt. D.S. Glover, P.T.H. Green collection)

The School of Aerial Gunnery, based at Palmarsh aerodrome, near Hythe became No. 1 (Auxiliary) School of Aerial Gunnery, part of which operated from Lympne from January 1917, as the Advanced Air Firing School. To aid the trainee gunners of the Royal Flying Corps to polish up their skills before going overseas, one of the air firing targets, held here by Sgt. Fred Young, was towed behind this modified Be2E. (Sgt. F. Young)

No. 120 Day-bomber Squadron of the RAF had been formed at Lympne on 1 January 1918, but also flew the services' air mail from Hawkinge to Maisoncelle in November 1918, using DH9As. On 1 July 1919 the service was transferred to Lympne until the RAF's involvement was finally terminated in August. A sergeant checks bags of mail as they are loaded into the rear cockpit of D1216, which has been fitted with a temporary cover. (RAF Museum No. P2511)

The Cornell family from the nearby village of Stanford had three sons who were serving in the Royal Flying Corps, one of whom was given a 'home posting' to the airfield at Lympne after being wounded while serving in France. He was a mechanic, and one of the main tasks he would have undertaken was the assembly and testing of the aircraft which were delivered to the airfield, such as this Royal Aircraft Factory-built Fe2D. (E. Cornell)

This DH9A G-EAHF was a civilianized medium-bomber flown by Messrs Air Transport & Travel Ltd, which took over the mail flights until August 1920, and would also carry freight and newspapers. Occasionally passengers would be carried on the return flights, for a £3 single fare. (Sgt. F. Young)

This Blackburn Kangaroo G-EADG, a converted maritime reconnaissance bomber, was being used for joy-riding by the Grahame White Air Service at Lympne in 1919. The Kangaroo was also used by the North Sea Ariel and General Transport Co. for their short-lived Leeds–Lympne–Amsterdam passenger and freight service, from 6 March 1920. (J.M. Bruce, M.A.P.)

Light Aviation Trials
1923, 1924 & 1926

Much interest was generated by the 1923 Light Aviation Trial at Lympne in 1923, attracting the then Duke of York (later King George VI) and Sir Samuel Hoare, who are seen here inspecting the Air Navigation and Engine Co.'s entry. The pilot did not have any view forward, only sideways, while a hinged glazed panel gave access to the cockpit. (KAHRS archives)

After the derequisition of Lympne, the next event of any significance was the Light Aviation Trials, which were held at the airport in 1923, 1924 and 1926. This was an attempt to find the ideal design for a flying club aircraft, promoted by the Air Ministry and sponsored by the *Daily Mail*. The 1923 competition, which included tests for endurance, speed, manoeuvrability and reliability, was for single-seater aircraft with an engine of 750cc capacity. This gave the designers some headaches, as this minimal power could only just lift aircraft, a pilot and fuel.

The 1924 and 1926 competitions were for two-seater designs with dual control, and the engine size finally increased to 1,500cc. In the event none of the ingenious designs submitted by established firms, such as Avro, Blackburn, Bristol, Handley-Page, Parnall and Short Brothers, or the one-off machines built by smaller firms or private enterprise, provided design potential which led to large-scale production, although the Avro Avian, Blackburn Bluebird and Westland Widgeon did enter production, but with larger capacity engines.

The Air Navigation & Engineering Co.'s ANEC 1 was one of the more unusual entrants for the *Daily Mail* 'Motor Glider Competition' of 1923. Designed by W.S. Shackleton, the pilot sat in a hammock seat below the wing with only a view upwards and to each side, via cut outs in the fuselage. Despite this it came second overall. (Aircraft Photographs)

Geoffrey de Havilland entered two of his DH53 designs in the 1923 competition – No. 8 'Humming Bird' (seen in the hangar) flown by Capt. de Havilland and Hubert Broad, and No. 12 'Sylvia' by Major Hemming. Powered by the 750cc Douglas motorcycle engines, their raucous noise was muted by a long exhaust pipe. (F. Cruttenden)

The Gloster Gannet, a neat little biplane, with only 18-ft wing span, was the entry from the Gloucestershire Aircraft Company for the 1923 Trials. However, major cooling problems with its specially designed Carden two-stroke engine prevented it from taking part in the competition. (Aircraft Photographs)

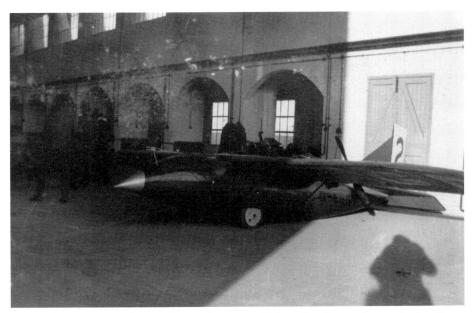

The bird-like Gnossepelius Gull was the entry of Short Brothers, who retained a flying facility at Lympne until 1929 for testing their land plane designs. Two machines were entered for the 1923 contest but were plagued with problems, mainly the over-heating of the 698cc Blackburn engine buried in the fuselage (F. Cruttenden)

Among the more unconventional entries for the 1923 Light Aviation Trials was the RAE Hurricane G-EBRS with its triangular section fuselage, thick tapered wing and wheels mounted inside the fuselage. But it persistently flew 'tail down' and had an unreliable special 600cc Douglas engine, so did not achieve its full potential. (B. Sherran)

The Avro Avis appeared in two designs for the 1924 trials, powered by either a Blackburn three-cylinder radial (No. 10) or a Bristol Cherub (G-EBKP), both versions being flown by Bert Hinkler, well-known Australian long-distance pilot. Due to engine vibration, both of the machines could only be flown at half throttle. (J.M. Bruce/C.S. Leslie collection)

DH51 G-EBIM visited Lympne during the Light Aviation Trials of 1924, and showed the progress towards the design of the ultimate flying club aircraft, the DH60 Moth. The DH51 was later fitted with single-bay wings and was flown in the 1925 King's Cup Race by Capt. C.H. Barnard. (F. Cruttenden)

The Air Navigation & Engineering Company's ANEC IV was an adaptation of their 1923 entry, with an extended wing and second cockpit. Powered by a 1,100cc Anzani engine, it was flown by racing pilot J.H. 'Jimmy' James. It was eliminated after suffering a broken valve spring in the qualifying tests. (J.M. Bruce/C.S. Leslie collection)

The Beardmore WB XXIV Wee Bee was similar in design to the ANEC IV, both being the work of W.S. Shackleton, then working at the Beardmore Company of Dalmuir, Glasgow. Again, this design was aimed at the elimination of drag, with a fully cantilevered wing and direct-drive Bristol Cherub engine giving an excellent speed of 86 m.p.h. During the 1924 trials it performed well until the last day, when it was obliged to complete the remaining laps for the distance competition. Having completed five laps, it was forced down with big end trouble only two miles from the finish line. However, the nearest competitor also failed to finish, so the Wee Bee gained the £2,000 first prize. (P. Jarrett)

The Blackburn Aeroplane and Motor Company's Bluebird G-EBKD was one of the more successful light aircraft designed for the 1924 competition. It featured side-by-side seating for pilot and pupil, and was sturdily built along the line of the torpedo-carrying aircraft that the company built for the Royal Navy. Although it was not ready to take part in the 1924 contest, it was re-engined and slightly modified for the 1926 competition, but was eliminated during the preliminary tests with a damaged undercarriage. (RAF Museum No. P6376)

The Bristol Aeroplane Company entered two of their Brownies for the 1924 competition. Mainly of metal construction, one had timber wings, the other being all metal. After a problem with wing 'flutter' on the wooden-winged Brownie it was eliminated, but C.F. Uwins, piloting the No. 1 machine, was successful in attaining second prize thanks to a good speed, good take-off, slow flying and distance performance. It maintained its winning ways two years later, gaining a third place in the 1926 competition. (RAF Museum No. 6534)

One ingenious solution from Parnall designer Harold Bolas for the 1924 competition was the Pixie. Although the company had three entries (Nos. 17, 18 & 19) these were in fact two monoplanes, with a detachable upper wing to convert them into biplanes for certain tests. (J.M. Bruce/C.S. Leslie collection)

The scrutineers insisted that all three entries should be presented together for checking, so entry No. 18 disappeared from the list, the two Pixies being flown in their biplane form as IIIAs. However, both of them were eliminated during the preliminary speed tests with engine problems (J.M. Bruce/C.S. Leslie collection)

The Vickers Vagabond 16 was a two-seater version of their Viget of 1923, and a larger and heavier machine powered by a Bristol Cherub III engine, flown by Rex Pierson as in the previous year. Due to engine vibration the Vagabond was not able to complete the elimination tests. (J.M. Bruce/C.S. Leslie collection)

The Westland Aircraft Works of Yeovil entered both monoplane and biplane designs for the 1924 competition. Their Woodpigeon was a fairly conventional biplane design, but although it completed all the elimination tests successfully, it did not distinguish itself in the competition proper. (J.M. Bruce/C.S. Leslie collection)

The Westland Wigeon was the monoplane version of the Westland Woodpigeon, but featured an unusual trapezoid wing design to give the pilot a better upward view. Powered by a Blackburn three-cylinder radial engine, it was eliminated when its wing-tip struck the ground, as the pilot was forced down by a strong north-easterly wind in the lee of the ridge near Postling. By coincidence, some time later, its stable companion was similarly obliged to land at the same spot, but without damage. (RAF Museum No. P9302)

The Hawker Cygnet was designed by Sidney Camm, who was later to design many of the firm's aircraft, including the Hurricane. Like the Avro Avis, two were entered in the 1924 Light Aviation Trials. No. 14 was powered by a 1,100cc Anzani, and No. 15 by an ABC Scorpion. Both entrants were eliminated, but one was declared the winner of the 1926 competition. (J.M. Bruce/C.S. Leslie collection)

Designed by R.J. Mitchell, later of Spitfire fame, the Sparrow was a 'sesquiplane' – the lower wing being narrower than the top one. Flown by Supermarine's test pilot, H.C. Baird, it had the misfortune to suffer a forced landing on the first circuit of the speed tests, thus eliminating it from further competition. (J.M. Bruce/C.S. Leslie collection)

SECTION THREE

Visitors: 1919–1939

An aerial view of the foreign flying club aircraft attending the 1937 International Air Rally at Lympne, from the roof of the club hangar. Amongst the countries represented are France, Germany, Belgium and Switzerland. These international air rallies attracted a wide entry from all parts of Europe and beyond. (J.T. Williams)

Lympne Airport saw many visiting aircraft during its period of operations, and these ranged from the ultra-light aircraft such as the BAC Drone motorized glider to the stately four-engined biplane HP42 airliners of Imperial Airways. Its proximity to the coast enabled the international aviators a last opportunity to refuel before leaving on their cross-Channel flights.

Although the airport was designated as an HM Customs clearance point, it did not have a resident customs officer, so a quick telephone call to Folkestone Harbour was needed when his attendance was required. The perimeter of the landing field was marked and lit, a wireless station installed, and in 1930 a high-visibility 'aerial lighthouse' was erected to guide aircraft into Lympne at night or in poor visibility. When a departing aircraft took off, the French airfield at St Inglevert was advised, and if confirmation of its arrival had not been received within two hours, HM Coastguards were then advised.

The widest selection of foreign aircraft was to be seen at Lympne during the popular international air rallies organized by the Cinque Ports Flying Club in the 1930s. Club and private pilots would fly to Lympne from as far away as Scandinavia and Yugoslavia, although France, Belgium, Holland and Germany flying clubs were the main attenders.

The Avro 504K was the most popular mount for the joy-riding operations which were so popular between the wars, giving 'Five Bob Flips' to those who had never flown before. This Avro 504, which had been built from spares remaining from the First World War production lines, was used by Berkshire Aviation Tours Ltd in 1932. (F. Cruttenden)

Using the first production model DH61 Giant Moth G-AAEV, Sir Alan Cobham undertook a five-month propaganda tour from May to October 1929, visiting towns and cities to promote municipal airports. As well as hundreds of schoolchildren, he gave some 3,500 mayors, and members of corporations, flights in his ten-seater aircraft, 'Youth of Britain', as part of his campaign. (F. Cruttenden)

The development of the original Blackburn Bluebird was the Mk IV G-ATTO, here being refuelled at Lympne. The aircraft was sold in 1930 by Auto Auctions Ltd, Heston, to Mr Norman Holden of Selsey, reverting to the manufacturers at Brough in January 1932. It was later destroyed in a fatal crash at nearby Broomfield. (F. Cruttenden)

The Blackburn Aeroplane and Motor Co.'s ultimate side-by-side training aircraft was their all-metal constructed B2 which featured Alclad covering. Registered to North Sea Aerial and General Transport Co. Ltd in April 1934, G-ACLD survived the war to take part in the 1947 Folkestone Aero Trophy race at Lympne. (F. Cruttenden)

The Robinson Redwing appeared in May 1930, and although built in small numbers at Croydon by the Robinson Aircraft Co. it was never to compete with the Moth. G-ABLA was the first production machine to appear, and was registered to the Wiltshire School of Flying Ltd at High Post aerodrome in October 1931. (F. Cruttenden)

A successor to the ubiquitous biplane Moth, the De Havilland DH94 Moth Minor was developed under the personal aegis of Sir Geoffrey de Havilland. First flown in June 1937, it proved as popular with flying clubs, and G-AFRR attracted plenty of attention when visiting Lympne just before the outbreak of the Second World War. (F. Cruttenden)

The DH84 Dragon was a mini-airliner developed for a London–Paris (via Ramsgate) service at the request of Mr Edward Hillman. This example was registered to the Hon. Brian Lewis in April 1933. Leased to Highland Airways, Inverness, G-ACCE crashed on take-off from Kirkwall on 29 August 1934. (F. Cruttenden)

Another mini-airliner was the Short Scion 2, being designed by Short Brothers of Rochester, although production was later transferred to Pobjoy Aircraft and Airmotors. G-ADDP was acquired by H.G. Thynne in April 1938, and remained at Lympne until sold to Williams & Co. at Squires Gate, Blackpool, in May 1939. (R.L. Giles)

The Chilton DW1 G-AESZ was the prototype lightweight air racing aircraft, developed in 1937 as a cheap, easy to maintain, private owner aircraft, and visited Lympne for that year's air racing. Powered by a 32hp Carden-Ford modified car engine, a Chilton DW1a won the Folkestone Aero Trophy in 1939. (Mrs A. Davis)

The forerunner of today's helicopters was the autogiro. The Cievra C-30A G-ACWR was one of the first batch of production aircraft and was privately owned by J.G. Weir, until it was sold to the Autogiro Flying Club in March 1939. It was photographed at the Lympne International Air Rally on 28 August 1936. (R.L. Giles)

The Bristol F2B Fighter, seen here being refuelled at Lympne, was a two-seater fighter, communications and Army Co-Operation aircraft with the RAF, continuing in main line service at home until 1922, and soldiering on with specialist and auxiliary units until the late 1920s. (F. Cruttenden)

An example of a Fleet Air Arm aircraft visiting Lympne is this Fairey IIIF Mk III communications and spotter aircraft S1845, and it was probably *en route* from an aircraft carrier to shore base. The III series served both at home and overseas, the float plane version being based at RAF Westgate near Margate towards the end of the First World War. (F. Cruttenden)

The Fairey Aircraft Company also built this neat Fox II light bomber in 1925. Powered by the American-built Curtis D12 engine it was faster than most fighters. Many were exported and this machine (G-ABFG/ex J9834) was photographed at Lympne while *en route* to the Royal Belgian Air Force in 1930. (F. Cruttenden)

These two Bristol Bulldog fighters were going abroad to the Swedish Air Force in 1932 (two crowns of the markings can be seen above the lower starboard wing). Entering RAF service in May 1929, Bulldogs represented some 70 per cent of the United Kingdom's fighter defences until replaced by the Gloster Gladiator in 1937. (E.A. Gower)

The Handley-Page Heyford B1 long-range bomber, which entered service with the RAF in 1933 and equipped eight front-line squadrons until replaced by the Whitley and Wellesley in 1937. Although of all-metal construction, they were still open-cockpit biplanes and were relatively slow with a top speed of only 142 m.p.h. One feature of the Heyford was a gap between the lower wing and the fuselage, bombs being carried in the thickened centre section. (Mrs A. Davis)

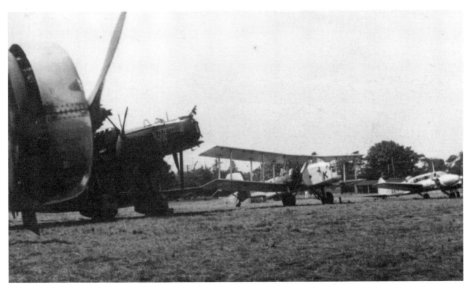

This example (K5193, of No. 10 Squadron) was present at Lympne for the Empire Air Display in May 1937, together with the Boulton & Paul Overstrand and an Avro Anson, representing the transition from the biplane bomber era. (Mrs A. Davis)

The Boulton Paul Overstrand B1 was a medium bomber flown by No. 101 Squadron, based at Bicester from 1934 until 1937, the year that K4453 attended the Empire Air Day at Lympne. The first RAF bomber to feature a power-operated gun turret, and replaced by the Bristol Blenheim, they remained in service until 1941 as gunnery trainers. (Mrs A. Davis)

This Avro Tutor K3426 of the Oxford University Air Squadron was on display at the 1937 Empire Air Day at Lympne, and was representative of the numbers of both University and Royal Auxiliary Air Force squadron aircraft which used the airport for their annual summer camps from 1927 until the outbreak of war. (R.L. Giles)

Representing the modern RAF, this Avro Anson K8742 from No. 224 Squadron at RAF Manston, was also present at the 1937 Empire Air Day at Manston. It equipped both Nos. 48 and 206 squadrons, the School of Air Navigation and No. 500 Squadron RAAF, which were all based at Manston from 1936. (Mrs A. Davis)

This Hawker Hind (K4936) two-seater day bomber of the London University Air Squadron came to grief whilst landing at Lympne during the annual squadron camp of 1939. Two regular RAF squadrons equipped with these Hawker Hinds (Nos 21 and 34) were based at Lympne from October 1936 until the summer of 1938. (R.L. Giles)

Attended by the airport fire engine (a converted Second World War armoured car), this Avro Tutor T1 K3363 of the London University Air Squadron lies on its back at the airfield after a landing accident, while measures are taken to right it. This is just one of many such minor incidents which occurred while auxiliary units undertook intensive training at Lympne, during the hectic months of the summer of 1939. (R.L. Giles)

The entrance to Lympne airport in the 1920s, with the doors to the first pair of hangars marked 'Continental Arrivals and Departures' as they were used by Imperial Airways to house their airliners. The large white object on the right of the photograph is one of the boundary lights. (J. Gilham)

Vickers Vimy Commercial G-EASI of Instone Airlines was one of the first airliners used on the London–Paris route, being a civilian version of the firm's well-known transatlantic bomber. This aircraft force-landed in fog on the cliffs by the Valiant Sailor public house near Folkestone, in August 1923. (T. Mitchell)

The Armstrong Whitworth Argosy had three engines for safety on the cross-Channel route, and was first ordered by Imperial Airways, entering service in 1924. They continued in service until replaced by giant Handley-Page HP42s in 1933. Flying to all parts of Europe, the aircraft were named after famous cities. (Mrs B. Pembroke)

The Dutch equivalent of the Argosy was this Fokker FVII/3m which was a development of the single-engined FVII, the three engines being preferred on long-range flights. This Fokker 00-AIT was flown by SNETA, one of the Belgian airlines which was amalgamated with others to form the national airline SABENA. (F. Cruttenden)

This Fokker FVII 00-JUB was registered in Belgium, and was used by SABENA for early morning newspaper delivery flights to Lympne, with the occasional passenger. It is photographed in the visitors' hangar at Lympne, while undergoing some repairs in 1927. On the return flights it usually only carried the pilot's washing! (E.A. Gower)

Another visitor is this French Farman F20 Goliath airliner of Air Union which, like SABENA, started early morning newspaper flights in 1923 from Paris, with single-engined aircraft. Unlike the Argosy and the Fokker FVII/3m the Goliath relied on only two engines for the Channel crossing. (F. Cruttenden)

One of the first German airliners to fly into Lympne was this three-engined Junkers G31 D-1786, distinguished by its curious tail configuration. From the anxious-looking crowd gathered under the wing, it might be assumed that the landing may have been caused by an engine problem of some kind. (F. Cruttenden)

A very smart-looking Junkers Ju53/3m airliner D-ALAM of the Geman airline Deutsches Lufthansa photographed at Lympne in 1938, posed with the prototype Currie Wot (see p. 96). The structure which is perched atop the end of the hangar is the dish aerial used for the high-speed radio link with St Inglevert. (T. Osbourne)

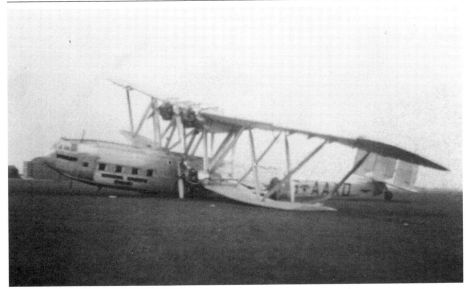

Handley-Page HP42 G-AAXD 'Horatius' which damaged its undercarriage during a forced landing at Lympne in September 1938, all the passengers and crew being unhurt. The aircraft was repaired in one of Lympne's hangars and continued its career with Imperial Airways until it crashed in 1939. (Mrs A. Davis)

This photograph shows the usual practice of painting out the company name (sometimes even before passengers had been disembarked) to avoid any adverse publicity before the press photographers arrived, so keen were Imperial Airways to preserve their reputation for reliability and safety. (Mrs A. Davis)

The Carmichael 'Microray' was the invention of the resident Marconi Company wireless engineer based at Lympne during the 1920s to speed up wireless communications, and predated the UHF satellite dishes of today. Lined up with a similar dish at St Inglevert, radio messages could be transmitted quickly, advising of the departure of airliners crossing the Channel. The Lympne dish was mounted on the brick door guides of the Cinque Port Flying Club's hangar overlooking the airfield. (RAF Museum P5374-4)

A wolf in sheep's clothing. This Royal Aircraft Factory SE5A G-EBXC (registered in Germany as D 1635) was dispatched via Lympne in May 1929. This aircraft was first registered to Major J.C. Savage of the Savage Skywriting Co. Ltd, who had had it converted for aerial advertising, which was popular in the 1920s. (F. Cruttenden)

Photographed at Lympne one frosty morning, this German-built Espendaub parasol wing design monoplane D-1859 had just been delivered from Germany. It was never registered in Britain, as it was later to crash near the airport on 8 December 1930, injuring the pilot, a Mr Farqueson. (F. Cruttenden)

An example of a Belgian-built aircraft is this Bulte RB30 00-ALY parked outside the Imperial Airways hangar at Lympne, in 1936. Constructed by Avions Bulte et Cie of Wolventen near Brussels in the 1930s, it was destroyed by enemy action during the German advance through Belgium in May 1940. (F. Cruttenden)

Another Belgian-registered aircraft to visit Lympne, although designed in France, was this St Hubert monoplane 00-AKL, constructed by Jose Orta of Club d'Aviation, at Brussels in the 1930s. It may not have survived the war, as it was removed from the Belgian Civil Aircraft Register in April 1946. (F. Cruttenden)

This French-built Caudron C193 G-ABFX was the sole example to appear on the British Civil Aircraft Register, having formerly been registered as F-AJSI when in France. Privately owned by Harold Swann at Heston, it was sold abroad in June 1931 after only seven months in the UK. (F. Cruttenden)

Another French-built import was Potez 36 F-ALJC which was to become G-ABNB on the British Register, although it never carried these marks. It was used for joy-riding with C.H. Barnard's 'Flying Circus' after arriving at Lympne in June 1931, but it was found unsuitable and was returned to the manufacturers at the end of the season. (F. Cruttenden)

One of the most peculiar aircraft ever to visit Lympne must have been this Focke Wulf 'Ente' (Duck) D1850, which was a 'canard' or tail-first monoplane. This layout was used in an attempt to eliminate stalling when the nose of the aircraft was raised to too high an angle, causing instability. The second example built by the company, it came to England for demonstration flights in November 1931 but did not find any purchasers, although it attracted considerable curiosity. (R. Humphreys)

This Northrop Delta 1C monoplane G-AEXR was a non-starter in the 1934 MacRobertson race to Australia. Plans to use it for a long-distance flight by Mrs Beryl Markham in 1937 were unfulfilled. Seen here at Lympne with (left to right) Tony Law, Ann Davis and Mr Wellman, before export to Iraq. (Mrs A. Davis)

Major George de Sevensky and his family visited Lympne in February 1939, where he demonstrated his new monoplane fighter (which would eventually evolve into the P74 Thunderbolt) while on a tour of European countries. Here, Mrs Ann Davis poses with Major and Mrs Sevensky before they leave for the Continent. (Mrs A. Davis)

Built during the First World War, this 1916-vintage Hanroit biplane 00-APJ was visiting Lympne in 1937, where the pilot shows off its peculiarities to an admirer. Registered in Belgium, this single-seat fighter was also used by the Belgian, Swiss and Italian Air Forces and some were built in the USA. (Mrs A. Davis)

Even older was this 1912 Caudron Trainer, which was imported for the Nash Collection, and delivered via Lympne in 1938. It was the cause of much interest at that year's International Air Rally. Aircraft such as these had been used for pilot training in the early years of the First World War by the Royal Navy Air Service. (Mrs A. Davis)

SECTION FOUR

Air Racing
1920–1939

Amongst the entrants for the annual air races held at Lympne in August 1938 were Percival
Mew Gull G-AEKL and Gull Six G-ADFA, Hendy Hobo G-AGIG, Chilton DW1s G-AFGH
and ESZ, Comper Swift G-ABUS, Short Scion G-ADDP and Hornet Moth G-ADMT, the latter being the winner of the Folkestone Aero Trophy that year. (Mrs A. Davis)

Air racing at Lympne in 1923 was initiated by Lord Edward Grosvenor, who presented a
challenge cup for British light aircraft to be flown by British pilots. This proved popular as
it excluded the 'souped-up' ex-RAF machines and foreign entries, and was aimed at the
private pilot. In the years of the Light Aviation Trials, the competitions for both distance
flown and speed were held as races, usually on a triangular course from the airport to
Postling, South Hill near Brabourne and back to Lympne, a total of some 12.5 miles.
When the Folkestone Aero Trophy (1932) and the Wakefield Cup (1933) races were insti-
tuted a new course was introduced, consisting of an alternative route to the airship shed
on the cliffs at Capel-le-Ferne, the Folkestone Harbour lighthouse, the Hythe town gas-
works gasometer and back to Lympne.

Lympne had the distinction of hosting the last major air race meeting to be held in the
UK before the outbreak of hostilities, when the Folkestone Aero Trophy was competed for
on 5 August 1939.

The Light Aviation Trials of 1924 included a race for RAF service aircraft for the Air League Challenge Cup. One of the Sopwith Snipes from No. 32 Squadron crashed after hitting some telephone wires along the airfield boundary. Despite the extensive damage to the aircraft, the pilot was unhurt. (KAHRS archives)

This Sopwith Scooter G-EACZ was piloted by J.C.P. Phillips in the Royal Aero Club Race Meeting held at Lympne from 1–3 August 1925. As there were no Light Aviation Trials planned that year, many of the previous year's contestants were entered for the races, as well as more conventional designs. (Photographs Co. Ltd)

The RAE Hurricane G-EBHS was entered by Flight Lieutenant J.S. Chick, who was placed first in the Light Aeroplane International Holiday Handicap on Saturday 1 August 1925. He also won the 100-mile Grosvenor Challenge Cup Race, and the Private Owners' Race on the Bank Holiday Monday. (J.M. Bruce/C.S. Leslie collection)

Although not completed in time for the 1924 Aviation Trials, the Cranwell CLA3 G-EBMC, did appear at the Royal Aero Club's Air Races held in August 1925. Designed by Flt. Lt. 'Nick' Comper, it was the predecessor of his successful series of light aircraft, including the ubiquitous Swift. (B. Sherran)

Dr Edward Whitehead-Reid in the cockpit of his SE5A G-EBCA which he entered for numerous race meetings from 1920 to 1930. Sometimes he entered anonymously as his wife did not relish the thought of him flying. This photo may have been taken at the Private Owners' Race on Monday 3 August 1925, in which he came second. (W.G. Whitehead-Reid)

Built by the Austin Motor Co. Ltd in 1919, the Austin Whippet G-EAPF was disposed of when the company relinquished its aircraft interests in 1923. Eventually purchased by Flt. Lt. F.O. Soden, it was entered in the 1925 August Bank Holiday race meeting at Lympne, but was unplaced. (J.M. Bruce/C.S. Leslie collection)

The Armstrong-Whitworth Siskin was one of the RAF's fighter aircraft that took part in air racing during the 1920s. This Siskin Mk II, a two-seat trainer version (G-EBEU), was usually flown by Capt. Frank T. Courtney. He visited Lympne for the 1925 August Bank Holiday race meeting, after which he gave a demonstration of aerobatic flying. Courtney also piloted the Parnall Pixie when he returned to Lympne for the 1926 Aviation Trials, in which it gained fourth place overall. (RAF Museum No. P2723)

The Gloster Grebe was another RAF front-line fighter of the 1920s, No. 25 Squadron based at RAF Hawkinge being the first to be completely re-equipped with the type. This example (J7520) is the two-seater trainer version of the Grebe, that was flown to victory in the 1929 King's Cup Race by Flt. Lt. R.L.R. Atcherley (entered as R. Llewellyn) with Flt. Lt. G.H. Stainforth as navigator. One of the control points for the race was at Lympne that year. (RAF Museum No. P7255)

The route for the 1929 King's Cup Race included a new checkpoint at Lympne, where members of the newly-formed East Kent Flying Club assisted with marshalling and refuelling. Seen in this photograph is the De Havilland Aeroplane Co. service van, which was kept busy: no less than half of the entries were that company's aircraft! (F. Cruttenden)

Watching out for the next arrival. The East Kent Flying Club helpers had to cope with rather a strong wind on the exposed airfield, and oil drums were used for picketting down the machines to prevent them being blown over. The aircraft is one of the three Avro Avians entered for the race. (F. Cruttenden)

There were twenty entries for the new Folkestone Aero Trophy Race held on 25 August 1932, including this American Monocoupe 110 two-seat side-by-side cabin monoplane. Registered as G-ABDR it was hurriedly repainted after being initially marked as G-ABBR. It gained third place at an average speed of 110.5 m.p.h. (T.W.J. Solly)

The winner of the Folkestone Aero Trophy was Mr A.J. Styran in his 120hp Gipsy III-engined Comper CLA7 Swift G-ABWH, entered by the British Air Navigation Company of Heston. In the background is the Puss Moth G-ABIJ entered by Sir Philip Sassoon, who was the Hon. Under Secretary for Air, hence the red, white and blue tail stripes. (T.W.J. Solley)

The second prototype Miles M2 Hawk G-ACHJ was specially built for Sqn. Lr. H.M. Probyn, D.S.O., C.O. of No. 25 Fighter Squadron, in 1933. Whilst based at Hawkinge he was often an entrant in races at Lympne, where he won the 1933 Cinque Ports Wakefield Cup Race at an average speed of 115.5 m.p.h. (F. Cruttenden)

One of the series of Miles racing aircraft built between the wars, this Hawk Major G-ADGE was entered in the 1937 Wakefield Cup Race held at Lympne. Amongst the sixteen entries were French, German, Belgian and one Yugoslav machine. The winner was Herr Clausen in a Klemm K135 D-EHNE, and B. Karlis in VEF J-12 YL-ABG was second. (R.L. Giles)

This Hendy 302 G-AAVT was flown in the 1930 King's Cup by Capt. E.W. Percival, and may have prompted him to design his series of Gull cabin monoplanes, but although averaging 141 m.p.h. he was not placed. It was later re-engined and redesigned before appearing again at Lympne, and was withdrawn from use at Gravesend in 1938. (F. Cruttenden)

Captain Geoffrey de Havilland entered the 1937 Wakefield Cup Race with his De Havilland TK2 G-ADNO, which had been constructed by the apprentices at the firm's Hatfield works. On this occasion he only gained sixth place at 171.5 m.p.h. but the TK2 was raced to success at many more pre-war air races (R.L. Giles)

The finals for the Folkestone Aero Trophy Race was held at Lympne on 30 July 1938, with eight starters. Amongst them was this rakish-looking Percival Mew Gull G-AEKL, flown by Flying Officer David Llewellyn. But the race winner, on handicap, was Hugh Buckingham in a DH87 Hornet Moth biplane G-ADMT. (R.L. Giles)

Amongst the entrants for the 1938 Folkestone Aero Trophy was this Belgian Tipsy S2 flown by Gp. Capt. E.L. Mole. Similar two-seater trainers were used for Civil Air Guard training at the Bekesbourne aerodrome near Canterbury. In the background can be seen a Chilton DW1, Miles Sparrowhawk and De Havilland TK2. (R.L. Giles)

Mrs Ann Davis presenting the Folkestone Aero Trophy to Hugh Buckingham for his win in the 1938 race; G. Samuelson in a Comper Swift was second and the De Havilland TK2 G-ADNO, flown by Geoffrey de Havilland was placed third. Of the remaining five finishers, W. Humble in Miles Sparrowhawk G-ACTE was fourth, and Tony Morris in Hobo G-AGIG was fifth. (Mrs A. Davis)

SECTION FIVE
Record Breakers
1928–1938

With the intense interest generated in long-distance flying in the 1930s, there was usually a newsreel ciné camera to record the arrivals and departures from Lympne. Here a British Gaumont Newsreel van films Harold Broadbent on arrival from Australia in April 1937, to be shown in the newsreel the following week. (Mrs A. Davis)

During the interwar years, many record-breaking flights either started from or were terminated at Lympne. An advantage was its elevated situation above Romney Marsh so that, on taking off to the south, the aircraft were already some 200 ft above sea level, and did not have to waste precious fuel climbing to the altitude before crossing the English Channel.

Great rivalry was generated between the pilots, especially C.W.A. Scott and Charles Kingsford-Smith, who would record their achievements by tossing pennies with stamps attached on to the ceiling of the Cinque Ports Flying Club. The husband and wife team of Amy and Jim Mollison were frequent visitors, both for solo and combined record attempts. Another lady pilot who used Lympne Airport was Jean Batten, who held several world distance records on the outbreak of the Second World War.

The first attempted long-range flight from Lympne was that of Wg. Cdr. E.R. Manning, who had a 50-gallon fuel tank installed in the front cockpit of his Westland Widgeon III G-EBRN. He left on 23 April 1928 bound for India, but had to abandon his flight after reaching Baghdad. (F. Cruttenden)

The Fokker FVIIA G-EBTS 'The Spider' was also used for a record flight to the Cape leaving Lympne at 5.30a.m. on 10 April 1930, piloted by C.H. Barnard and R.F. Little, with the Duchess of Bedford as a passenger. It reached Maitland Airport, Cape Town in a record 100 hrs flying time. (F. Cruttenden)

After lowering the UK to Australia record, leaving Lympne on 1 April 1931 in Gipsy Moth G-ABHY, Charles W.A. Scott returned in the same aircraft, now registered as VH-UQA. Having left Darwin on 25 May 1931, he arrived back at Lympne at 7p.m. on 5 June 1931 – in just over ten-and-a-half days. (Aircraft Photographs)

Photographed at Lympne in 1931, this American-built Lockheed DL-1 Vega Special G-ABGK was piloted by Glen Kitson and Owen Cathcart-Jones to Cape Town between 31 March and 6 April, in just under 6 days and 10 hours. Unfortunately Kitson was to be killed only a month later in a crash, while flying in South Africa. (F. Cruttenden)

This all-black De Havilland DH60G Gipsy Moth VH-UFT (formerly G-AHFT) was flown by James Allan Morrison for his second attempt on the Australia–UK record. Unable to locate Lympne airport on arrival, 'Jim' was obliged to land on the beach at Pevensey Bay in Sussex on 6 August – after 8 days, 19 hours and 25 minutes, a new record time. He later flew on to Lympne. (F. Cruttenden)

The Spartan A24 Mailplane G–ABLI was specially converted to carry two passengers in the cramped mail compartment, and was fitted with twin tail fins for its record flight to India. Named 'Blackpool', it left Squires Gate aerodrome on 15 June 1932 and arrived at Dringh Road, Karachi, in just under six days. (F. Cruttenden)

Mr C. Arthur Butler flew this long-range version of the diminutive Comper Swift G-ABRE, powered by a 75hp Pobjoy 'R' radial engine, to Australia where he was domiciled, in just over nine days. Starting from Lympne on 31 October he reached Darwin on 9 November 1931, having lowered C.W.A. Scott's record for the same route by just 102 minutes. The aircraft was later shipped back to the UK for Victor Smith's attempt on the UK–Cape record the following year. (RAF Museum No. P9692)

The husband and wife team of Amy (formerly Miss Amy Johnson) and Jim Mollison broke many records while flying both to and from Lympne airport in the 1930s. With them in the photo (on the right) is Captain Duncan Davis of Brooklands Aviation Ltd, which took over the Cinque Ports Flying Club in 1932. His brother W.E. 'Bill' Davis was the club manager until his death in 1938. (R.L. Giles)

Receiving a last minute check-over in the visitors' hangar at Lympne, DH80A Puss Moth G-ACAB 'Desert Cloud' was used by Mrs Amy Mollison for her flight to South Africa, in November 1932. Starting from Lympne on the 14th of that month, she arrived at Cape Town just over four-and-a-half days later, beating her husband's time by some 10 hours, 28 minutes, to gain the UK–South Africa record. On her return journey she also broke the record to the UK, despite encountering bad weather *en route*. (R. Riding)

One of the strangest stories concerning a record flight that was attempted from Lympne was that of William Newton Lancaster, who left Lympne at 5.38a.m. on 1 April 1933. Flying Avro Avian V G-ABLK he had hopes of lowering Amy Mollison's record to the Cape. Having landed at Oran to refuel, he took off the following day for Gao, landing twice to check his directions. He then disappeared and was discovered near his crashed aircraft by a French military motorized Sahara patrol in February 1962, some 170 miles south of Reggan in Algeria. (RAF Museum No. P519)

Harold F. Broadbent regained the Australia–UK solo record when he arrived at Lympne in his DH85 Leopard Moth VH-AHB fitted with special fuel tanks giving it an extended range of some 1,500 miles. He left Darwin on 27 April 1937 and arrived at Lympne on 3 May. (Mrs A. Davis)

Harold Broadbent, accompanied by his manager, walks towards the terminal at Lympne, where his official arrival time will be logged for the Royal Aero Club and his claim for the record will be entered. He made one more successful flight from Australia to England in Percival Vega Gull G-AFEH, in April 1938. (Mrs A. Davis)

Miss Jean Batten waves to the crowd on her arrival at Lympne after her record-breaking flight from Darwin in her Percival Gull Six G-ADPR at 3.45p.m. on 24 October 1937. She had gained the solo Australia–UK record (5 days, 18 hours and 15 minutes) as well as the record for female pilots. (J.T. Williams)

Winner of the Britannia Trophy for her record-breaking trip to South America in 1936, Jean Batten's success in gaining the records to both Australia and her native New Zealand in 1937 again won her the trophy for that year. A record of her flights was inscribed on the rudder of her aircraft when she arrived at Lympne. (R.L. Giles)

Cinque Ports Flying Club: 1928–1939

Lined up outside the club's own hangar in 1938, the aircraft represent the range of aircraft flown by the Cinque Ports Flying Club. In the foreground are two new BA Swallow 2s G-AEYW and AEVC; Leopard Moth G-ACPG flanked by DH60GIII G-ACHH (right); and DH60M Moth G-AAKP, with DH60G Moths G-EBTD, ABOG, AASF and ABWN in the rear. (Mrs A. Davis)

The origins of the club flying at Lympne started with the interest generated by the light aviation competitions, which led to the formation of the East Kent Flying Club in November 1927, after a meeting organized by Mr H.E. Twaites and Mr R. Dallas-Brett, a local solicitor. A company was floated and incorporated in February 1928, and it held a local exhibition to generate interest, as well as organizing a flying meeting that Easter. The club purchased two aircraft, appointed a ground engineer and flying instructor, and commenced training in May.

The East Kent Club proved popular and by 1931 membership stood at 220, but it struggled financially and on 1 January 1932 became part of Brooklands Aviation Ltd. It was renamed the Cinque Ports Flying Club. During the period until 1939, Lympne was one of the most popular venues for club flying, under the able organization of the then secretary Mr W.E. 'Bill' Davis and his wife Ann. The club formed its own maintenance unit, which became Cinque Ports Aviation Ltd, and took part in the Civil Air Guard training programme from 1938, giving subsidized lessons to pupils who intended to join the RAF if war broke out.

The first aircraft to be purchased by the new East Kent Flying Club was DH60X Moth G-EBWC, that was used for flying instruction from Easter 1928. The aircraft's registration letters were not very popular with lady members, who objected to its lavatorial connotation. Moves were made to have it re-registered as G-EBZN, but before this could be done it was taxied into the side of a hangar on 7 July and written off. (RAF Museum No. P1705)

The replacement for G-EBWC was another Cirrus Moth G-EBSS in July 1928, but this was lost in a fatal crash when a young pilot attempted to perform advanced aerobatics after only four hours' solo experience. He crashed at Selby Farm on Romney Marsh, just to the south of the airport, on 13 October 1928. (F. Cruttenden)

The second Cirrus Moth G-EBNN was purchased by the East Kent Flying Club on 22 September 1928, but like its predecessor it did not survive the rigours of flying club training, being badly damaged in an accident near Newingreen on 27 March 1929, while being flown by club instructor Major Travers. (F. Cruttenden)

This magnificently maintained Bristol Fighter G-ABYT had suffered from a heavy landing before being parked in the club's hangar, and was scrapped at Lympne, 16 July 1929. At one time it was owned by the popular Cinque Ports Flying Club instructor Mr K.K. Brown, who had become the club's third flying instructor in April 1929, having served with the RAF in No. 25 Fighter Squadron, based at Hawkinge. He later moved to the Kent Flying Club at Bekesbourne, near Canterbury. (R. Riding)

Resplendent in the official Cinque Ports Flying Club colours of silver, with black and orange zig-zags and pennant, is this DH60X Moth G-EBRI, which survived a crash in August 1928. It became one of the longest serving club machines, giving some 1,072 hours of trouble-free flying in the club's service. (F. Cruttenden)

Still wishing to update its equipment, the DH60X Moth G-EBSA was acquired by the Cinque Ports Flying Club on 23 May 1930, to join the Cirrus 1 Moths G-EBRI and EBQE still in commission. By October, however, all three had been exchanged for three new slotted DH60 Moths G-AAFS, AAKM and EBDT. (F. Cruttenden)

As well as the flying club machines, private owners would often hangar their personal aircraft at Lympne. One of these was this two-seater Hendy Hobo G-AAIG, which had been modified for air racing purposes after being acquired by club member Lord Patrick Crichton-Stuart, in 1934. (F. Cruttenden)

When they decided to acquire more modern training aircraft, the Cinque Ports Flying Club acquired both in-line and radial-engined versions of the British Aircraft Co. Ltd's Swallow 2 monoplanes. The 90 m.p.h. Pobjoy Cataract III-engined G-AEIH was the first registered to the flying club, in June 1936. (Mrs A. Davis)

The personal aircraft of Cinque Ports Flying Club secretary, 'Bill' Davis, was General Aircraft ST25 Monospar Universal G-AEJV, which was purchased as a wedding present by his wife, Ann. It was first registered to him in January 1937, also being used for ferry and charter work as well as joy-riding. (F. Cruttenden)

On 12 March 1938, Bill Davis took up some passengers for a flight in his Monospar at the end of the day, although joy-riding had already finished. On crossing the eastern boundary of the airport both the engines cut out, and G-AEJV crashed into a field opposite his own residence, Berwick House, with fatal results. (T.W. Osbourne)

A rare photograph of Bill Davis flying the prototype Currie Wot on the last flight before his fatal crash in March 1938. Designed as an aerobatic single-seater by J.R. Currie, who was a lecturer at the College of Aeronautical Engineering, Chelsea, it was built with the help of their students as a practical exercise in 1937. The aeroplane's name, it is rumoured, came about as its designer became irritated when he was constantly being asked 'What are you going to call it?' when designing his brainchild. (T.W. Osbourne)

The phototype Currie Wot G-AFCG, with the Cinque Ports Flying Club logo painted below the cockpit. This aerobatic single-seater was built for about £250, required just 50 yards for take-off, and cruised at 75 m.p.h., using only two gallons of petrol per hour. (Mrs A. Davis)

The second Currie Wot was G-AFDS. Both Wots shared the same 40hp Aeronca–J.A.P J99 twin-cylinder engine, from the wrecked Aeronca C3 G-ADZZ. Only two examples flew before the Second World War, but plans were made available for home-builders in the 1950s and several post-war examples have been constructed. (T.W. Osbourne)

The last of the biplanes, three Cinque Ports Flying Club Moths with DH85 Leopard Moth G-ACPG, the club 'hack' used for charter work as well as the flying club's air taxi. The Moths are (left to right) DH60X G-EBTD; DH60G G-ABOG and DH60M G-AAKP, the last of which was acquired in 1935. It was to survive until June 1940, when it was pressed into RAF service for use as an instructional airframe, with the Air Training Corps. (R.L. Giles)

To assist in the training of Civil Air Guard pupils in 1938, the club purchased two DH82 Tiger Moths, G-ACGE and G-ADWG, the latter arriving resplendent in black and white chequerboard paint after a season with C.W.A. Scott's flying circus. It was repainted in the Cinque Ports Flying Club's more sombre colour scheme, and was flown by them until the outbreak of the Second World War. This aircraft was exported to India as VT-AMA in January 1940. (R. Riding)

A group of Cinque Ports Aviation Ltd apprentices pose with one of the Percival Gull monoplanes which they were servicing in 1937. Mr Ron Giles was one of these apprentices, who learned to fly in his spare time with the Civil Air Guard while he was at Lympne. (R.L. Giles)

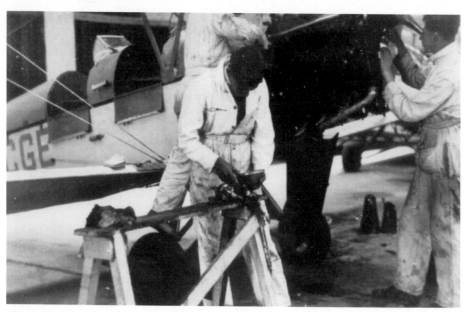

Three Cinque Ports Aviation apprentices working in the club hangar on Cinque Ports Flying Club's Tiger Moth G-ACGE in 1939, while being trained for their 'B' Licences, or Ground Engineer's qualifications. Some of them eventually went on to serve in the RAF or Fleet Air Arm during the Second World War. (T.W. Osbourne)

SECTION SEVEN

Some Lympne Personalities

What every private flyer was wearing in the inter-war years! Dr E.D. Whitehead-Reid of Canterbury, seated in the cockpit of one of his two SE5A civilianized RAF fighters that he used for air racing. A frequent visitor to Lympne, he was killed in a forced landing at dusk, at East Sutton Park, near Detling, Kent, in October 1930. (KAHRS archives)

The first Lympne personality to come to notice was probably Ken Waller, an Australian who had learned to fly at Lympne and progressed to be a well-known long-distance flying and air race pilot. The most popular flying instructor of the early years was Mr K.K. Brown, the club's third flying instructor.

When Mr W.E. 'Bill' Davis took over as secretary–manager in 1932, although not then a pilot, he quickly learned to fly with K.K. Brown. He then steered the club into world-wide popularity, ably supported by his wife Ann, in the six years before his tragic accident in March 1938. Mrs Davis bravely took over her late husband's post as flying club secretary and guided it through the difficult eighteen months before the outbreak of war.

The club was to lose another popular staff member in September 1938, when Flt. Lt. David Llewellyn was killed in BA Swallow G-AELI while instructing near the aerodrome.

Some of the staff of the Cinque Ports Flying Club in 1931, who include (left to right) Mr A. Baker (Assistant Ground Engineer), Mr K.K. Brown (Chief Flying Instructor), Mr G. Warner (Club Steward) and Mr R.H. Wynn (Ground Engineer). Mr Warner served at the club until 1939. (Mrs B. Pembroke)

A group of early flying club members: (left to right) Mrs Twaites (the wife of the club treasurer), Mr H.R. Law (son of prime minister Bonar Law), Mr K.H.F. Waller (later club flying instructor, air racer and long-distance record breaker), Mr D.A. Gill, Miss Jarman and Capt. R.A. Jarman. (Mrs B. Pembroke)

One of the most enthusiastic members of the flying club in 1930 was Mr D.A. Russel (right) seen with Mr H.R. Law and the latter's Blackburn Bluebird G-AABF. Mr Law was the first club member to attempt any long-distance flight from Lympne. This took place in January 1930, in his Westland Widgeon monoplane G-EBRN. (Mrs D.A. Russel)

Striding towards the club hangar is Chief Flying Instructor for the Cinque Ports Flying Club, Mr K.K. Brown, while the De Havilland Cirrus Moth is refuelled with Pratts High Test petrol from the club's own fuel pump. K.K. Brown was killed in a collision over Tilmanstone with an R Aux AF aircraft in 1939. (F. Cruttenden)

A group of Cinque Ports Flying Club instructors seated outside the club hangar, (left to right) Tom Hackney, Tony Morris, Tony Duport, with Messrs Rowbotham and Wallace. As well as a clubroom and bar, the club had a lean-to veranda built on the side of the hangar, overlooking the aircraft parking area. (Mrs A. Davis)

Some 'high jinks' involving club members in fancy dress, arresting Mr Albert Batchelor of the Thanet Aero Club. This may have been on a 'Dawn Patrol', when the host club tried to log the aircraft of visiting pilots before landing; those evading the logging got a free breakfast! (Mrs A. Davis)

The Duke of Kent and Princess Marina entering a red and blue Airspeed Envoy G-AEXX of the King's Flight, when departing from Lympne on 22 May 1937. They had been piloted by Wg. Cdr. Fielden, the O.C. of the King's Flight, while on a visit to Shorncliffe Barracks at Folkestone. (Mrs A. Davis)

A group of club members with Tony Duport (second left) who was also a director of Cinque Ports Aviation Ltd, which was formed initially to maintain the flying club's own aircraft. It was later to take on light engineering work on contract from other local firms, but never made much of a profit. (Mrs A. Davis)

Flt. Lt. David Llewellyn supporting the prototype Currie Wot, assisted by two Cinque Ports Aviation apprentices, for a publicity photograph. David Llewellyn was Chief Flying Instructor at Lympne when he was killed in an aircraft accident on 21 September 1938. He was a popular instructor and long-distance flyer, gaining the record from the Cape to Britain in November 1935 – holding this until the following year, when he was beaten by Flt. Lt. Tommy Rose. He also took part in many of the pre-war air races. (T.W. Osbourne)

Tom Hackney took over as the chief flying instructor after David Llewellyn's death. He is seen here relaxing outside the club's hangar between duties. The refuelling pumps, some newly-erected RAF huts, two of the club's BA Swallows and a Tiger Moth are in the background. (Mrs A. Davis)

When the R Aux AF Squadrons were camping at Lympne, contacts were made with the Cinque Ports Flying Club as shown in this group. Pat Umache, Lord Patrick Crighton-Stuart, and Mrs Ann Davis are socializing on the club's veranda with a contingent from the camp in 1937. (Mrs A. Davis)

A group of Cinque Ports Aviation Ltd apprentices in 1938 at Lympne, with directors 'Bill' Davis and 'Tony' Duport (fourth and fifth from the left in front row). Mr J.R. Currie (third from left) was a lecturer at the College of Aeronautical Engineering, Chelsea and some senior students received their practical training at Lympne over the weekends, including working on his Currie Wots. Mr Ronald Giles is at the right end of the centre row. (T.W. Osbourne)

Mrs Ann Davis at her desk in the office at Lympne, when she was running the flying club after the death of her husband. In 1946 she returned to Lympne to restart the flying club, before taking over the 'Bellevue' country club next door to the airport. (Mrs A. Davis)

Lord Patrick Crighton-Stuart flanked by Tony Duport and Ann Davis at the 1938 air races at Lympne. Lord Patrick's Hendy Hobo G-AAIG is in the background, being serviced by apprentices from the club's own maintenance organization. Tony Duport supported Ann in running both the flying club and Cinque Ports Aviation Ltd until its closure. The aircraft was stored at Lympne on the outbreak of war, but destroyed in the air raid of 15 August 1940. (D.C. Palmer)

Close ties were maintained with other flying clubs in the Brooklands Group, at Sywell, Northants and Shoreham, Sussex in a joint membership with Brooklands, Surrey. Here a group from the Brooklands club have flown into Lympne with Capt. Duncan Davis, for lunch, during the first week of July 1939. (Mrs A. Davis)

Mr Ron Giles, seen here in uniform with his 'wings' up after going solo in January 1939, was one of the engineering apprentices who had learned to fly at Lympne under the Civil Air Guard subsidized training flying scheme. It was started in 1938 to provide a reserve of trained pilots for the RAF in wartime. (R.L. Giles)

RAF and FAA at Lympne 1938–1945

An aerial view of Lympne airfield taken on 18 August 1942, showing the new 'blister' hangars which had been erected to replace those destroyed in August 1940. The Spitfires of No. 133 and 401 (RCAF) Squadrons were in occupation to provide some of the fighter cover for the Dieppe landings. (RAF Museum No W/13/1/8)

The RAF had reoccupied Lympne well before the Dunkirk evacuation, and several Army Co-Operation and bomber squadrons, as well as various stragglers, were received. During the Battle of Britain Lympne was virtually destroyed, and the airport was evacuated until mid-September. The first unit to return was a flight of No. 91 Squadron Spitfires, followed by the Hawker Typhoons of No. 1 Squadron. More Spitfires arrived to cover the Dieppe landings in August 1942, and the Typhoons returned, equipped with air-to-ground rockets, for strikes against the V-1 flying bomb launching positions across the Channel.

Many Allied aircraft found the airfield a safe haven when returning with battle damage and wounded crew members, while fighter squadrons carried out long-range escort duties with the RAF and USAAF bombers when on sorties into occupied Europe and Germany.

This Fairey Battle light bomber was photographed at Lympne during the annual air exercises which were held to test the defences of the UK each year until 1939. On the outbreak of war, Battle B1s were also delivered to the Advanced Air Striking Force in France. (E. Cornell)

The Fleet Air Arm arrived at Lympne after the airport had been commissioned as 'HMS Buzzard' on 1 July 1939. FAA machines such as this Blackburn Shark III K8899 were to be seen at the airport after the naval air mechanics' school was established there shortly afterwards. (R.L. Giles)

Although outclassed by the Luftwaffe's Messerschmitt Bf109s these Gloster Gladiator biplanes (seen refuelling at Lympne) were thrown into the Battle of France and undertook patrols off Dunkerque, together with Spitfires and Hurricanes, while the remnants of the British Expeditionary Force were evacuated. (R.L. Giles)

After the holocaust! An aerial view of the hangars and RAF camp at Lympne after the bombing raids of August 1940, which had badly damaged the station, especially the assault on the 15th of that month by Ju87 Stuka dive bombers of II/StG1. The three pairs of hangars were all hit, and that housing the flying club's aircraft which had not been evacuated to Sywell, in September 1939, was destroyed in a two-day blaze. The station

HQ was hit, the water supply cut off, and delayed-action bombs were scattered about the airfield. The station was out of action for 48 hours and was then only available for emergency use until mid-September, when this photograph of their handiwork was taken by the Luftwaffe. (USA archives, R. Humphreys)

After being found unsuitable for a twin-engined fighter, the Westland Whirlwind was converted to a fighter bomber, and used against Channel shipping and targets in the Pas de Calais area from May 1942 until June 1943. An example from No. 137 Squadron (then based at RAF Manston) in a blister hangar at Lympne. (B. Sherran)

Rocket firing Hurricanes of No. 137 Squadron arrived at Lympne in December 1943 to take part in extremely dangerous anti-ship strike operations, to deny the enemy passage of war materials carried in shipping convoys through the Straits of Dover. They left Lympne in the new year to re-equip with Typhoons. (B. Sherran)

A Hawker Typhoon 1A R8752 JX-L of No. 1 Squadron RAF after one of the all-too-frequent engine failures (often with fatal results) when this new design first entered service with an unreliable power plant. This particular example made its forced landing near Lympne on 2 June 1943. The squadron served at Lympne from March 1942 until February 1944, to deal with the new Focke Wulf FW190s over the English Channel. (Imperial War Museum No. CRH 18509)

Officers and NCOs of No. 1 Squadron pose in front of one of their Hawker Typhoon F1s while stationed at Lympne under CO Sqn. Ldr. 'Tony' Zweigberke. The Typhoon was a tight fit for the small airfield, one runway being extended over Otterpool Lane, while the

PSP (perforated steel planking) dispersals were situated in the north and south-east corners. During winter months the Typhoon's temperamental Sabre engine had to be run-up at intervals during the night, which was not at all popular. (L. Pilkington)

A Spitfire IX of the 403rd 'Wolf's Head' (Canadian) Squadron RAF at Lympne in 1944, with its pilot. Their Spitfire IXs were flown on escort duties for Typhoon fighter-bombers of No.

137 Squadron, who had moved into Lympne on 8 February 1944 to undertake bombing raids on the Continent, in preparation for the D-Day invasion of Europe in June. (C.H. Thomas)

Lympne became the recipient of many damaged British and USAF aircraft returning from sorties over Europe, short of fuel, suffering from battle damage and with wounded men aboard. This Boeing B-17G Flying Fortress of 379th Bomb Group landed at Lympne in February 1944. The arrival of large four-engined B-17s and B-24s was a constant headache for the Station Commander, as a belly-landing could block the main runway for hours. (C.H. Thomas)

The Typhoon fighter-bombers of No. 137 Squadron pose with their Spitfire escorts of No. 403 (RCAF) Squadron on the snow-covered airfield in February 1944. The Typhoons would be starting fighter-bomber work the following month, before leaving to convert for rocket firing attacks on targets along the French and Belgian coasts. Much of their work concerned the destruction of V-1 Flying Bomb launching sites in the Pas de Calais, and when this attack started in June 1944, squadrons based at Lympne played their part in combating this threat on London. (C.H. Thomas)

After August 1940, much of the accommodation at Lympne was dispersed, either to houses near the airfield, or into Lympne village. The NAAFI staff had been evacuated to the village hall when some of them were photographed in a copse along the Aldington Road, opposite the bungalow where Miss Irene Cannon was billeted, in December 1943. They are (left to right) May Tort (cook), Heather, -?-, Mrs Richardson (manageress), Myrtle, -?-, Queenie, Irene Cannon.

SECTION NINE
Post-War Civil Aviation: 1946–1968

Aerial view of Lympne c. 1948, showing two of the blister-type hangars (black), and the new Super Robin hangar (white) on the base of the old hangars and camp. Distributed around the terminal are some wartime buildings which were used by the flying club and airlines. In the foreground is the country club at 'Bellevue' run by Mrs Ann Davis. (P. Bamford)

When civilian flying resumed at Lympne in 1946 the airport had changed considerably since the Cinque Ports Flying Club aircraft had been evacuated in September 1940. The club commenced operations using the facilities remaining from the RAF's occupation, but only survived for two years. The Kent Gliding Club shared the airport for several years, while 1948 saw the start of the aerial photography operation by Messrs Skyfotos.

The Cinque Ports Flying Club was started again in March 1964 by Mr Barry Damon, and was immediately successful. It continued to flourish and by 1968 had 120 members training on imported Piper and Beech aircraft.

This De Havilland Tiger Moth G-AHNY formed part of the batch of aircraft flown by the re-formed Cinque Ports Flying Club in April 1946. Registered to the club in June 1946, it was reduced to spares in September 1948 when the club folded, due to lack of support from the government for post-Second World War club flying. It was photographed at the first post-war air race meeting held at Lympne in August 1946. (R. Riding)

The successor to the Cinque Ports Flying Club was the equally short-lived Kent Coast Flying Club formed by Wg. Cdr. Hugh Kennard in 1949. This Miles Magister G-AKJK was also flown from Ramsgate Airport, until it crashed at Lympne in July 1954. It is seen parked outside one of the wartime 'blister' hangars (usually known as the Walker and Thompson hangar after the firm who occupied it) at the old dispersal point on the south-east boundary. (R. Riding)

Auster J/1 Autocrat G-AIZZ also shared its times between both Lympne and Ramsgate airports in the late 1940s, while both were under the control of Wg. Cdr. Hugh Kennard. This aircraft was also used by Skyfotos, formed in 1948 for aerial photography, and specializing in photographs of international shipping passing through the English Channel. It was also the first aircraft to land at the reopened Ramsgate Airport in 1952. (Wg. Cdr. Hugh Kennard)

This American-built Piper PA 22 Caribbean G-AREN replaced an Auster of Skyfotos, which was lost while on a photo sortie. This aircraft was ditched off Beachy Head in the 1960s, with the loss of both pilot and photographer; the latter seen here standing by the aircraft before a sortie. (C . Hamilton)

The close proximity to the French coast meant that Lympne was used to the presence of various continental-registered aircraft, when arriving or departing from the UK. An example of these is this British-built but French-registered Miles Hawk Trainer 3 F-BDPH which was photographed at Lympne in the late 1940s. (F. Cruttenden)

One resident of Lympne at this time was British-built Christlea Super Ace 2 G-AKUV, 'Thursday's Child', registered by Mrs R. Morrow-Tait in 1948, who had intended to use it for an attempt on the round-the-world record. However, after it was damaged in a landing accident it was later rebuilt by Mr J. Chapman. (F. Cruttenden)

An unexpected arrival which didn't quite cross the airfield boundary was a Slingsby Sedburg glider which crashed on the Aldington Road in the 1950s. This may have been flown by a member of the Kent Gliding Club or by an ATC cadet up from the RAF Home Gliding Centre, then based at Hawkinge aerodrome. (T. Mitchell)

Although not the victim of a crash, this skeleton was all that remained of a De Havilland Rapide G-AKME, which was burnt out after an accident while being refuelled on 30 June 1950. Note a dark patch under the cockpit windows where the owner's name is painted out, just as had been done on HP 42 G-AAXD. (F. Cruttenden)

Another De Havilland Rapide to be written off at Lympne was G-AGOJ, which was owned by Mr Eric Rylands, the future founder of the Skyways airline. It remained there until 1961, when it was damaged beyond repair on 1 May. In the background is the structure of Lympne's second hangar under erection (T. Mitchell)

Also owned by Mr Rylands was this Avro XIX G-AGPG (note same logo on the fin as the Rapide P121) and, although rarely seen outside the hangar, it emerged on this occasion to give joy-rides to a party of handicapped children from a local school. The airport tractor had been used to mow the runway shortly before. (T. Mitchell)

Refuelling at the petrol pumps in January 1962 was this De Havilland Leopard Moth G-ACMA of J.P. Filhol Ltd, reviving a scene that would have been more familiar in pre-war days at Lympne. Incidentally this aircraft had originally been registered to a petrol-eum company, National Benzol Ltd, in March 1934. (DGC)

The Cinque Ports Flying Club was re-formed by Australian air enthusiast and pilot Mr Barry Damon in March 1964, at which time it was equipped with American Piper and Beech aircraft, and this German-designed and built Bolkow Monson. Some members of the new club are seen here with Mr Damon (third from the left). (C. Hamilton)

Members of the new Cinque Ports Flying Club were trained on this Beech Bonanza G-ARZN and Beech A23 Musketeers G-ATBI, VDP and WFZ. The long score on the grass runway is the aftermath of the forced landing by one of Messrs Skyways Avro 748s G-ARMV on the evening of 11 July 1965 (see pp. 152–3). (C. Hamilton)

More and more American-built aircraft were to be seen at the airport during the 1960s, including such types as this Cessna 172F G-AWUO, which was imported after assembly in France. On one occasion, before the raising of import duty, large deliveries of up to a dozen aircraft in formation landed at Lympne. (DGC)

Visiting Lympne for the opening ceremony of the new terminal in June 1969 was Miss Sheila Scott, in her Piper Commanche 260B G-ATOY 'Myth Too', after setting up her round-the-world record. She also gained those for female pilots for both North and South Atlantic crossings, as well as those to South Africa and New York. (DGC)

Also present was this Nord 1101 F-BLEJ, a French-built Me108 based on the Messerschmitt Bf108 light communications aircraft used by the Luftwaffe during the Second World War. Although many foreign aircraft visited the airport, especially during the annual Baden-Baden round-Europe air rallies, there were never as many as during the 1930s. (DGC)

Not a wartime photograph, but Ray Hanna's Spitfire MH464 at Lympne for the occasion of the one and only 'air rally' event held at the airport post war. The occasion was a Garden Party Open Day organized by the new Skyways International airline after their management buyout of the original Skyways in June 1971. (DGC)

After Messrs Dan Air, Business Air Travel, Skyfotos and the Cinque Ports Flying Club vacated Lympne in October 1974, the activity at Lympne was severely reduced, but in July 1983 this Piper Super Cub, adapted for glider-towing (hence the registration) was in residence at a small flying club/joy-riding establishment. (DGC)

The Eagle Parachute School was also in residence for a short time before removing to Headcorn. The small flying club operation was struggling to maintain a commercial presence at Lympne at this time, joy-riding being given in this Piper Aztec G-TEFC – again an appropriate registration for the flying club. (DGC)

SECTION TEN

Air Racing Revival 1946–1950

Air racing returned to Lympne when the first post-Second World War event was held at Lympne over the weekend of 31 August/1 September 1946, with heats for the Folkestone Aero Trophy being run on Saturday. Both pre-war biplanes were restored to their former glory and the modern single-engined monoplane trainers competed. (D.C. Palmer)

In 1946 the series of annual air races was re-instituted at Lympne, a novelty being the new High Speed Handicap Race. This was open to British and foreign pilots flying aircraft with a minimum handicap speed of 270 m.p.h., in what was claimed to be the fastest ever air race to have been held in Europe.

The Folkestone Aero Trophy was restored to the UK air-racing calendar, having been presented to the Cinque Ports Flying Club by Mr Walter Bentley in 1932 for competition between pilots from British and foreign light aeroplane clubs. Races for similar types of aircraft were also part of the programme, the ever popular Tiger Moths and their post-war equivalents, the Miles Magisters and Proctors, being featured.

Handicapped by Messrs Rowarth and Dancy, seen checking Marz Sokol M1A OK-AAH away at the start of the Folkestone Aero Trophy Race, the first seven aircraft in the heats on Sunday were the finalists in the race on the following day. The course was the same as that flown in pre-war races. (D.C. Palmer)

One of the pre-1939 registered entrants was Tipsy Trainer 1 G-AFJT, formerly owned by Air Vice Marshal Sir Arthur Longmore, and now being flown by D.R. Robertson. In the background are a Percival Proctor, a pre-war BA Swallow 2, a new Miles Messenger and the Czech-built and registered Marz Sokol M1A. (D.C. Palmer)

Winner of the Folkestone Aero Trophy in 1946 was this Supermarine Walrus amphibian G-AHFN of United Whalers, flown by John Grierson at an average speed of 121 m.p.h. The slowest entry was generously handicapped. Hugh Kennard in his Miles Messenger was second and J. Arnold, piloting a Proctor, third. (D.C. Palmer)

A race for Percival Proctors, the civilian version of a Second World War communication aircraft of the RAF, also formed part of the afternoon flying programme. Three of them are seen here in close formation just after take-off, including G-AHFZ, piloted by Sqn. Ldr. G.A. Reston, G-AHMV by D.M. Bay, and G-AHEE by J. Arnold. (D.C. Palmer)

The race for the Siddeley Trophy for flying club machines, in conjunction with the Folkestone Aero Trophy, was amended to a special race of thirty miles, as no flying club machines had qualified for the final. The winner was Cinque Ports Flying Club De Havilland Tiger Moth G-AHNX flown by R. Pomphret. (D.C. Palmer)

Second in the Siddeley Trophy Race was this pre-war Miles M2 Hawk Major G-ADCV, entered by the Wolverhampton Flying Club and flown by R.R. Paine. Although this pre-war activity was to be repeated in the following two years, no further air races were to be held at Lympne after 1948. (D.C. Palmer)

The highlight of the meeting was the Lympne High Speed Handicap flown over three laps by the entrants, all four of which were new fighter aircraft, some of them flown by the company test pilots. Seen here are (left to right) the DH100 Vampire F1 jet-fighter (second), the winning Hawker Fury F1, and the nose of the Supermarine Seafang F32 (fourth). (A.J. Moor)

In the 1947 Lympne Air Races a De Havilland Vampire F1 VF332 was flown by Grp. Capt. John 'Cats Eyes' Cunningham to sixth place in the Lympne High Speed Handicap Race at 494.63 m.p.h. The prize for the winner was the Hythe Aero Trophy, presented by the citizens of that town, and a cheque for £100. (B. Stickles)

A two-seater Spitfire Mk VIII Trainer attained fourth place in the High Speed Handicap Race at Lympne over the August Bank Holiday weekend in 1947, flown by Sqn. Ldr. W.J. Guy Morgan. The same aircraft returned the following year to win the trophy, when G-AIDN was flown by Flt. Lt. J. Colquhoun. (B. Stickles)

Sqn. Ldr. Guy Morgan returned to participate in the Lympne High Speed Handicap Race of 1948, flying the latest marque of Spitfire F24 VN324, seen here waiting his turn to take off. The High Speed Race was run over the old course to the Capel Airship hangar, to Folkestone Pier and the Hythe gas-holder. (B. Stickles)

A Tiger Moth Scratch Race was flown as part of the programme during the 1948 August Bank Holiday air races at Lympne. The entrants included machines from the Fairoaks Aero Club, the London Aeroplane Club, the Cinque Ports Flying Club (flown by Tom Hackney), and Air Kruise Ltd (flown by Wg. Cdr. Hugh Kennard). (B. Stickles)

Another race for one-class machines was that for Magisters, and all four contestants started together, as for the Tiger Moth race. After flying three laps around a five-mile course, which kept them in view of the spectators most of the time, the first one past the control tower was declared the winner. (B. Stickles)

Although not participating in any races at the airport, some of the contestants in the *Daily Express* South Coast Air Race arrived at Lympne before the contest on 16 September 1950, when a number of them were photographed at the airport. The pilots would have stayed at the Lympne Country Club. (J. Harrod)

One of the more ancient vintage machines competing in the race was this beautifully maintained 1932-vintage Comper Swift G-ACTF being flown by R.E. Clear from Christchurch, Hants. In the background can be seen a Percival Proctor 3 G-ALMS, which was to be flown by K.C. Millican. (J. Harrod)

Local resident and Silver City Airways employee, John Harrod, photographed his wife Pamela (right) and her friend Winifred Clark, standing by one of the pre-Second World War Miles racing aircraft taking part in the *Daily Express* Air Race, with a refuelling 'bowser' in the background. (J. Harrod)

This Percival Proctor 5 G-AHIT 'Windmill Girl' was entered by the owner of the Windmill Theatre, Vivian Van Damme, and was flown by Mrs Zita Irwin. Appropriate artwork, depicting a scantily clad female, is painted on the cowling, and is being admired by a friend of John Harrod, Mr Ted Harrington. (J. Harrod)

As well as using this Miles M65 Gemini 1A G-AKKB for air racing, it was also flown by Fred Dunkerley to set up six new records for outwards, return and round trip flights to Brussels and The Hague in June 1953, and a further four similar records to Dublin and Belfast during the following month. (J. Harrod)

This American-built Fairchild 24W-41A Argus 2 G-AJAT was flown by Miss Joan Hughes, who was one of the Air Transport Auxiliary pilots who delivered aircraft from factories to airfields during the Second World War. In the background can be seen Miles Falcon Six G-AECC, to be flown by Sqn. Ldr. J. Rush. (J. Harrod)

An overall deep blue colour scheme was featured by this Second World War Hawker Hurricane Mk IIC G-AMAU 'The Last of the Many', flown by Sqd. Ldr. F. Murphy. Although one of the fastest entrants in the South Coast race of 1950, it was severely handicapped, and therefore was unable to gain a prize. (J. Harrod)

A two-seater ab initio trainer about to enter service with the RAF was this Boulton Paul Balliol T2 VR602, one of the first production batch and flown by A.E. Gunn. The Balliol was later to serve with No. 7 Flying Training School and the RAF College, Cranwell. Like the Hurricane, it was unplaced. (J. Harrod)

The winner of the 1950 South Coast Air Race was this Proctor 1 G-AHUZ 'Nicodemus', flown by Nick Charlton at a speed of 164 m.p.h. From the number of suitcases which are being loaded into the cockpit, it might be assumed that at least this pilot had come well prepared to spend the night at Lympne Country Club. (R. Riding)

SECTION ELEVEN

Commercial Aviation
1948–1974

This Air Kruise Christmas card of 1948 featured one of their DH89A Dragon Rapides departing from Lympne airport at dusk, with the old wartime control tower silhouetted against the evening sky. This tower, which was situated on the highest point of the airfield, was later replaced by a more modern structure. (J. Gilham)

The commercial development of Lympne airport post war was undertaken in two distinct phases, that of Silver City Airways from 1948 to 1954, and that of Skyways Coach-Air/Dan Air between 1955 and the closure in 1974. Silver City had started their car ferry operations in July 1948 after moving from Blackbushe, Surrey. They eventually moved to a new purpose-built ferry airport at Lydd on Romney Marsh at the end of the 1954 summer season.

Lympne airport was offered for sale, but there were no bidders. Mr Eric Rylands leased the site and started his Skyways London to Paris 'coach-air' service, using three Douglas Dakota aircraft, in April 1955. In 1971 a management buy-out of Skyways prolonged the inevitable decline, but after Dan Air had taken over operations the following year, Lympne airport was living on borrowed time.

Photographed at Lympne in 1947 was this Bristol 170 Mk 21 Freighter of Messrs Air Contractors, one of the first of this type of specially designed freight carriers to be seen at Lympne. They were to become quite familiar in the following years when Silver City Airways started their car ferry service from Lympne. (B. Stickles)

East Anglian Flying Services Ltd operated this Miles Aerovan G-AJKM from Southend airport from 1947, seen loading passengers at the recently reopened Lympne airport. Unfortunately it was later damaged beyond repair, when it was blown over while being refuelled at Lympne in a gale, on 3 May 1949. (F. Cruttenden)

Wg. Cdr. H.C. Kennard, managing director of Air Kruise (Kent) Ltd taking delivery of the first civilian Miles Messenger 2A G-AHZS from Mr Mayo of Miles Aircraft Ltd in August 1946. This company later operated from Lympne flying a scheduled airline service to Le Touquet as Trans Channel Air Services Ltd, until they removed to Ramsgate airport in 1953. The company also undertook charter work and flew joy-riding operations from the airport. (H.C. Kennard)

The most important post-war event at Lympne was the loading of a 16hp Armstrong Siddeley car aboard the Bristol 170 Mk 1E Freighter G-AGVC on 13 July 1948. This was the inauguration of the first cross-Channel vehicle service to Le Touquet by what was soon to become Silver City Airways. Closed during the winter months, demand for car spaces increased every summer, resulting in the erection of another hangar at Lympne to house the firm's expanding fleet of Bristol Freighter car carriers. (R. Riding)

Viewed from under the port wing of a Silver City Freighter, the passenger facilities at Lympne were rather basic in the early days, mostly consisting of former wartime RAF huts. On the extreme left is the Ministry of Civil Aviation office; on the right are the airport fire engine and the crash truck. (J. Harrod)

Having arrived from Le Touquet, this pilot has parked his De Havilland Rapide G-AEWL, and waits while a member of the Air Kruise ground staff accompanied by Mrs Audrey Kennard propels the 'air steps' towards the aircraft to allow the passengers to disembark. Air Kruise took their Rapides to Ramsgate in 1953. (J. Harrod)

Wg. Cdr. Kennard (in sports jacket) with some of the pilots of Silver City Airways, watching cars being loaded on to one of their Bristol Freighters on the concrete apron. One of Air Kruise's Dragon Rapides is in the background. To his left is an Automobile Association staff member, on hand to assist the disembarking motorists. (O. Peck)

A wartime relic was this nissen hut, which served at the Forward Reception Centre and housed the offices of both the AA and RAC, to cater for car passengers. This photograph is interesting for the number of VIPs and officials present on this occasion: Chief Traffic Superintendent John de Wolfson is at the rear (in cap). (O. Peck)

In March 1953, Silver City took delivery of the first of the production run of the Bristol 170 Mk 32 Super Freighters, G-AMWA being the first of six to be purchased by the company for their expanding traffic from Lympne. It is seen here with one of the older Bristol 170 Mk 21 Freighters used originally in 1948. (Mrs P. Curd)

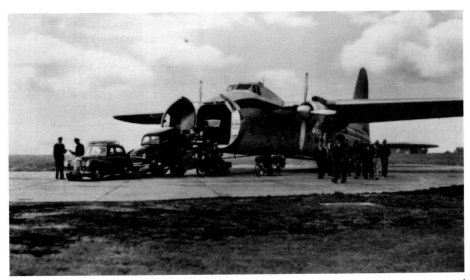

A publicity postcard issued by Silver City Airways to advertise the carrying capacity of their larger aircraft. A third car was only just accommodated in the elongated nose section of the Bristol 170 Mk 32 Super Freighter, which entered service in Lympne in the summer of 1953. (R. Woodward)

In the summer of 1953 a new car-ferry service was opened to Ostend using the new Mk 32 Superfreighter which could carry three cars and a motorcycle or two. Cars were charged, according to length, from £7 10s. 0d. single fare, bicycles at 5s. and passengers at £2 for a single fare. This photograph shows the close links which Silver City Airways

maintained with the motoring organizations such as the AA and RAC, with this representative load made up of the former organization's vehicles. This was obviously a publicity photo which would have been used to promote the new service, but by the following year the airline was no longer operating from Lympne. (J. Funnel)

One of the most popular of the Lympne air hostesses, both with passengers and staff, was Pat, seen here posing by the air crew room – attempts having been made to brighten things up with blinds and window box. The board behind her advertises Air Kruise's services, one of whose pilots she was later to marry. (O. Peck)

As with any small company, use was made of the staff for a publicity photograph, with company executive and airport manager Dick Dougall, with his wife and son posing on the steps of the passenger lounge to advertise the pleasures of travelling across the Channel with Silver City Airways (O. Peck)

Some of the ground staff working at Lympne for Silver City Airways included this fine body of men – only ground marshals and not pilots, despite the rakish angle at which their caps are being worn. There was no shortage of ex-RAF air or ground staff in those days immediately after the end of the Second World War. (O. Peck)

Communications at Lympne were in the capable hands of these 'gals' who worked in the telephone and telex operations room in 1954, handling bookings and flight schedules. At this time, as with the other facilities at Lympne in the 1950s, the accommodation was also a relic of the previous RAF occupation. (O. Peck)

After Lympne's temporary closure following the departure of Silver City to Lydd in October 1954, the airport remained unsold, so Mr Eric Rylands started his 'Coach-Air' service from London to Paris, via Lympne and Beauvais. Passengers travelled from Victoria coach station in East Kent buses. (The East Kent Road Car Co. Ltd)

Messrs Skyways utilized Douglas Dakotas G-AMSM and MWW, converted ex-USAF transport aircraft, that Silver City had also introduced for their passenger services in 1953. By contrast, in the foreground is the British-registered, Dutch-designed Tipsy Nipper light aircraft, a post-war version of the Flying Flea. (DGC)

The new Avro 748 turboprop airliner was introduced into the cross-Channel coach-air services in April 1962, and during the summer months both Dakotas and Avros were kept busy. An opportunity for refurbishment of the facilities was undertaken. (DGC)

Another Avro 748 (G-ATML) was added to the Skyways fleet in 1968 when it was leased from LIAT for this and the following season, to cope with increased bookings. Although it carried Skyways logo, markings and lettering, it still remained primarily in the original owner's colour scheme. (DGC)

The disadvantages of operating modern aircraft from a pre-1920 airport with grass runways culminated in a spectacular accident to Avro 748 G-ARMV, while landing on the evening of 11 July 1965. On touching down the nose wheel dug into the soft ground and the aircraft flipped over on to its back, careering some 400 yards upside down and tearing

off the port wing. Fortunately none of the passengers or crew was seriously hurt, but the aircraft was a write-off. Plans for the construction of a new concrete runway were then put in hand. (R. Woodward)

A new concrete runway was constructed during the winter of 1966–7 and was first used at Easter the following year. Aligned NW/SE it was some 4,400 yards long with turning circles at either end. Here Avro 748 G-ARRV, with turboprops whistling, and belching out paraffin exhaust fumes, lines up ready for take-off. (DGC)

After the financial crisis of 1970, a management buyout was arranged, giving a temporary respite to Skyways, re-formed as Skyways International Ltd. However, by 1972 a successful bid had been made by Dan Air, and after that year Avro 748s, painted in their red and white colour scheme, were to be seen operating from Lympne. (DGC)

My Last Day at Lympne

'Foxtrot Victor' was the radio call-sign of the last Bristol Freighter that Trevor Clapp was to fly from Lympne in September 1954. A Bristol 170 Mk IIA G-AIFV had first been registered in India with Dalmin Tain Airways in December 1946 as VT-CID, reverting to Indian National Airways in May 1947. It returned to the UK register for Silver City Airways in March 1950, having been upgraded to a Mk 21 Freighter. Seen here in full Silver City Airways colours in 1952, 'Foxtrot Victor' was withdrawn from use at their Ferryfield airport at Lydd airport in October 1961. (R. Nicholls)

My last day at Lympne in September 1954 started, as usual, with technical checks on the aircraft at first light, about 7.15 a.m., to be ready for the first flight of the day to Le Touquet. Passengers are waiting outside the Forward Operations and Reception building, while their vehicles are loaded ready for their departure at 0900hrs. In the background on the right can be seen the airport's refuelling station (T. Clapp)

After taxi-ing down the concrete ramp on to the grass in front of the passenger terminal, 'Foxtrot Victor' is guided into position by the senior car marshal at 8.05. In the background are (left) main airport reception building and offices by main gate. The HM Immigration and Emigration, HM Customs, Police and Special Branch and the AA and RAC accommodation is on the right. (T. Clapp)

By 8.15 'Foxtrot Victor' has the nose doors open to receive the motorized ramp for loading of vehicles. The Silver City colour scheme was silver overall, including the company name on fuselage stripes, aquamarine blue trim along the fuselage and for rudder stripes. Registration letters on tail fin and under port wing in blue, with the last two letters repeated in silver on the blue nose stripe. (T. Clapp)

Here I am posing for the last time in the uniform of Silver City Airways in front of Freighter G-AMFV 'Foxtrot Victor', giving an impression of the vastness of the Bristol Freighter Mk 21, on which I gained my first-ever air experience before joining the Fleet Air Arm later that year. This particular aircraft was lost in the making of the Jack Hawkins film *Man in the Sky*. (T. Clapp)

Easy does it, as another holidaymaker's vehicle is driven up the ramp into the hold of the Silver City car ferry as vehicle loading starts. This mobile car ramp had to be manhandled into position, and then jacked up to the exact level of the aircraft floor before loading of the vehicles. The passengers were accommodated towards the rear of the aircraft. (J. Harrod)

The last view from the perimeter track of 'Foxtrot Victor' as it is taxied on to the runway, seen from the public viewing gallery. It is in between one of the new Bristol Mk 32 Super Freighters, which were just coming into service, and is parked outside the reception building, and an Auster J/1 Autocrat G-AIGP that has been parked on the grass reserved for visiting light aircraft. (T. Clapp)

On hand to witness the return of the 'historic' last flight were Valerie Maskell (now Mrs Trevor Clapp) and her schoolfriend, Shirley Hickman. Seated in the public viewing area near the main gate, they await the arrival of 'Foxtrot Victor' from France with the return 10 a.m. service from Le Touquet. In the background can be seen one of the original buildings, the old RFC guardroom, which survived until recently, a reminder of the important part that the former Lympne Airport once played in the history of British aviation. (Mrs V. Clapp)

Acknowledgements

Messrs Aircraft Photographs • Mr Peter Bamford • J.M. Bruce/C.S. Leslie Collection • Mr Trevor Clapp • Mrs Valerie Clapp • Mr E. Cornell • Mr Frank Cruttenden • Mrs Ann Davis collection • *Flight International* • Mr John Funnell • Mr Ronald L. Giles • Mr John Gilham • Mr E.A. Gower • Mr Peter T.H. Green • Mr Charles Hamilton • Mr John Harrod • Mr Roy Humphreys • Imperial War Museum • Mr Phil Jarrett • Mr Stanley King • Wing Commander H.C. Kennard • Military Aircraft Photographs • Mr Terry Mitchell • Mr Tony Moor • Mr Rex Nicholls • Mr T.W. Osbourne • Mr D.C. Palmer • Mr O. Peck • Mrs B. Pembroke • Mr Len Pilkington • Real Photographs Co. Ltd • Mr Richard Riding • Mr Bruce Robertson • The Royal Air Force Museum • Mrs D.A. Russel • Mrs I. Shaw • Mr Brian Sherran • The Shuttleworth Trust • Mr T.W.J. Solly • Mr B. Stickles • Mr C.H. Thomas • Mr John Viner • Mr W.G. Whitehead-Reid • Mr John T. Williams • Mr Russell Woodward Sergeant Fred Young.